JANUARY
PATTERNS, PROJECTS & PLANS

by
Imogene Forte

Incentive Publications, Inc.
Nashville, Tennessee

Illustrated by Gayle Seaberg Harvey
Cover by Susan Eaddy
Edited by Sally Sharpe

ISBN 0-86530-129-8

Table of Contents

PREFACE

January – the start of a brand new year

JANUARY...

...A TIME of expectancy and promise — New Year festivity fills the air, resolutions are made and goals are set, young and old reminisce and look forward to a year of happiness and prosperity.

...A TIME of winter landscapes — snow covers hillsides and clings to tree branches, icicles hang from rooftops and windowsills, brilliant shining stars illuminate somber winter skies.

...A TIME of "wintertime" things — building snowmen, throwing snowballs, riding sleds down icy hills, drinking hot chocolate, sitting by the fire, curling up with a good book.

All of this and more is the excitement of January! Watch students' smiles widen and their eyes brighten as they enter your "come alive" classroom. Your classroom will say "January is here!" from the ceiling to the floor, from windows and doors, from work sheets and activity projects, from stories and books, and especially from you — an enthusiastic, "project planned" teacher!

This little book of JANUARY PATTERNS, PROJECTS & PLANS has been put together with tender loving care to help you be prepared to meet every one of the school days in January with special treats, learning projects and fun surprises that will make your students eager to participate in all phases of the daily schedule and look forward to the next day. Best of all, the patterns, projects and plans are ready for quick and easy use and require no elaborate materials and very little advance preparation.

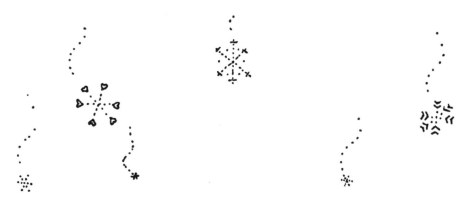

For your convenience, the materials in this book have been organized around four major unit themes. Each of the patterns, projects and plans can be used independently of the unit plan, however, to be just as effective in classrooms in which teachers choose not to use a unit approach. All are planned to complement and enrich adopted curriculum schemes and to meet young children's interests and learning needs.

Major unit themes include:
- January's Joys
- Birthdays Are Special Days
- Snow And Ice And Freezing Cold
- Learning About Clothing

Each unit includes a major objective and things to do; poster/booklet cover, bulletin board or display; patterns; art and/or an assembly project; reproducible basic skills activities; and book, story and poem suggestions to make the literature connection.

A special mini-unit on listening skills also is included which may be effectively correlated with the study and celebration of the New Year.

JANUARY'S JOYS

Major Objective:
Children will develop understanding of New Year resolutions and will develop awareness of the colors, sights, sounds and events that characterize the month of January.

Things To Do:

- Lead a discussion about New Year resolutions. Print the title "Our New Year Resolutions" on a large chart. As the discussion progresses, ask each child to tell one thing he or she plans to do during the year. Record the resolutions on the chart. Keep the chart in a reading corner for free reading and discussion.

- Send the "letter to parents" (page 10) home to announce the month's activities and to ask for donations for your materials collection. Check your supplies to be sure that you are ready for the month!

- Reproduce the positive communicators on page 25 and distribute them at appropriate times during the month. The beginning of the new year and the discussion of resolutions makes January the perfect time for positive reinforcement.

- Use the patterns in this book to make decorations for doors, windows, desks, etc.

To complete the activities in this book, you will need:

construction paper (assorted colors)	large 12-month calendar
crayons & markers	simple musical instruments (pg. 27)
paste	envelopes
scissors	ingredients for recipes (pg. 48)
tape	materials for bird feeders (pg. 59)
tissue paper (white & other colors)	materials for instruments (see pgs. 31-32)
silver wrapping paper	materials for experiments (pg. 60)
pencils	fabric scraps & articles of clothing
stapler	(pgs. 63-66)
drawing paper	dried beans
several small boxes	index cards
popsicle sticks	tape recorder & cassette tape

Dear Parents,

January is here, and that means it's "back-to-school" time once again! Many fun and exciting things to do and learn are in store for your child during the coming weeks.

This month our class will be learning about New Year resolutions and will make resolutions of our own! We also will study and celebrate the importance of birthdays as well as learn about cold winter weather and clothing.

In order to help with our projects, you can collect and contribute discarded clothing suitable for dress-up, scraps of fabric, shoe boxes and birthday decorations. Please feel free to suggest good books, poems and fairy tales for January reading. We'd love to have you join us for story time!

Sincerely,

JANUARY ALPHABET

A ... A new year has begun!
B ... Birthdays to celebrate
C ... Chilly winds
D ... Days are shorter
E ... Everyone bundles up!
F ... Fires aglow
G ... Going back to school
H ... Hot chocolate with
       marshmallows
I ... Icicles, shiny and cold
J ... Jolly snowmen
K ... Knitted sweaters to keep us warm
L ... Learning about clothing and
       cold weather
M ... Mitten magic
N ... New Year's Day
O ... Only a few months until spring!
P ... Pairs of socks and pairs of shoes
Q ... Quiet, still landscapes
R ... Resolutions to make
S ... Snow-covered landscapes
T ... Tree limbs covered with ice and snow
U ... Umbrellas for bad weather
V ... Vivid stars illuminate winter skies
W ... Winter days
X ... X-tra time for indoor play
Y ... Yahoo! It's snowing!
Z ... Zipp, zipp, zipping on sleds
       and skates

JANUARY

Sunday	Monday	Tuesday	Wednesday	Thursday	Friday	Saturday

HOW TO USE THE JANUARY CALENDAR

Use the calendar to:

...find out on what day of the week the first day of January falls
...count the number of days in January
...find the number on the calendar which represents January
...mark the birthdays of "January babies" in your room
...mark special days

- New Year's Day (January 1)
- Martin Luther King, Jr.'s Birthday (January 15)
- Benjamin Franklin's Birthday (January 17)
- National Handwriting Day (January 23)
- etc.

CALENDAR ART

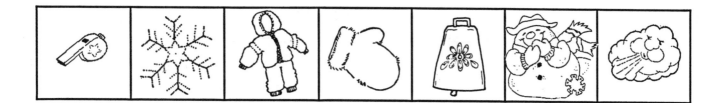

JANUARY MANAGEMENT CHART

CLASSROOM HELPERS

_____

is a bell-ringing
student!

_____

signed

Classroom
Messenger

♡
Dear

_____,

Welcome back
to school!
I missed you.

_____

signed

Teacher's
Helper

JANUARY DOORKNOB DECORATION

Color and cut out this doorknob decoration.
Hang it on your door to spread New Year cheer!

Happy
New Year
To You.

Construction:

1. Reproduce the bell patterns on pages 20 and 21. Cut two large bells out of silver wrapping paper. Color the other bells with markers or cut them out of construction paper.

2. Cut the caption "Bells Are Ringing For The New Year" out of construction paper.

3. Assemble the board as shown above.

4. Display stories, drawings, poems, songs and other seasonal items on the board.

Variations:

- **Bells Are Ringing For Good Books:** Display the children's illustrations of their favorite wintertime books.

- **Bells Are Ringing For Reading, Writing And Math:** Display the children's work on the board.

- **Ring A Bell For Our Class:** Have the children draw self-portraits on bell patterns to add to the board.

Prepare this bulletin board in December and have a head start on back-to-school preparation in January!

Construction:
1. Reproduce two copies of the bell pattern on page 20 and color the bells with markers or cut them out of construction paper.
2. Cut the caption "Ring Out The Old Year With Good Health Habits" out of construction paper.
3. Display the children's illustrations of good health habits on the board.

PREST-0, CHANGE-0!

Attach samples of the children's work to bell show-offs (page 22) and substitute the caption "Ring In The New Year With Your very Best Work" to turn a December bulletin board into a back-to-school bonus board!

LARGE BELL

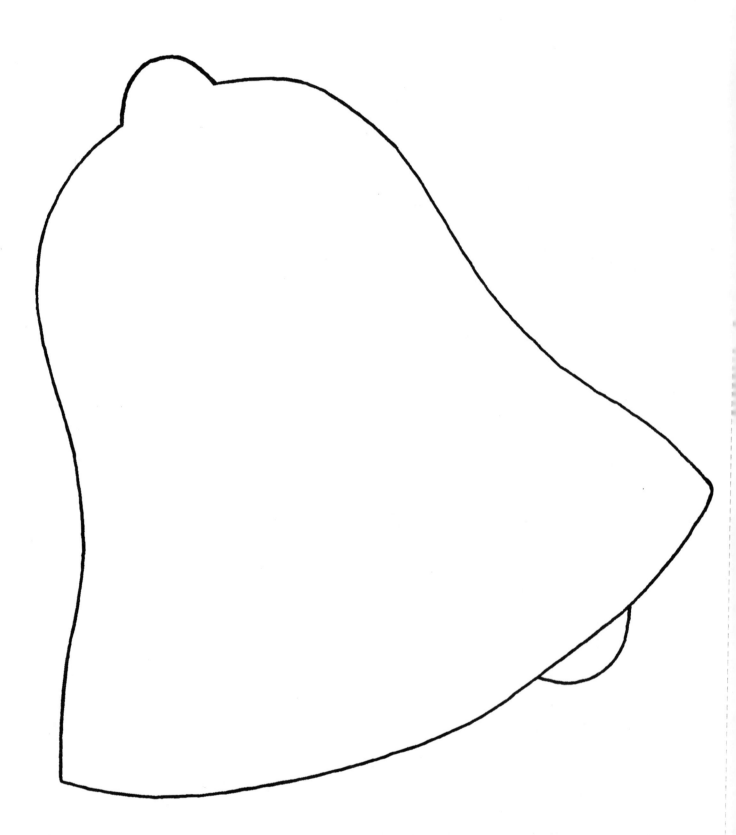

BELLS

21

BELL SHOW-OFF

To "show off" good work, help the children color and cut out bell show-offs to attach to their papers. Show-offs make attractive bulletin board displays and great "take homes"!

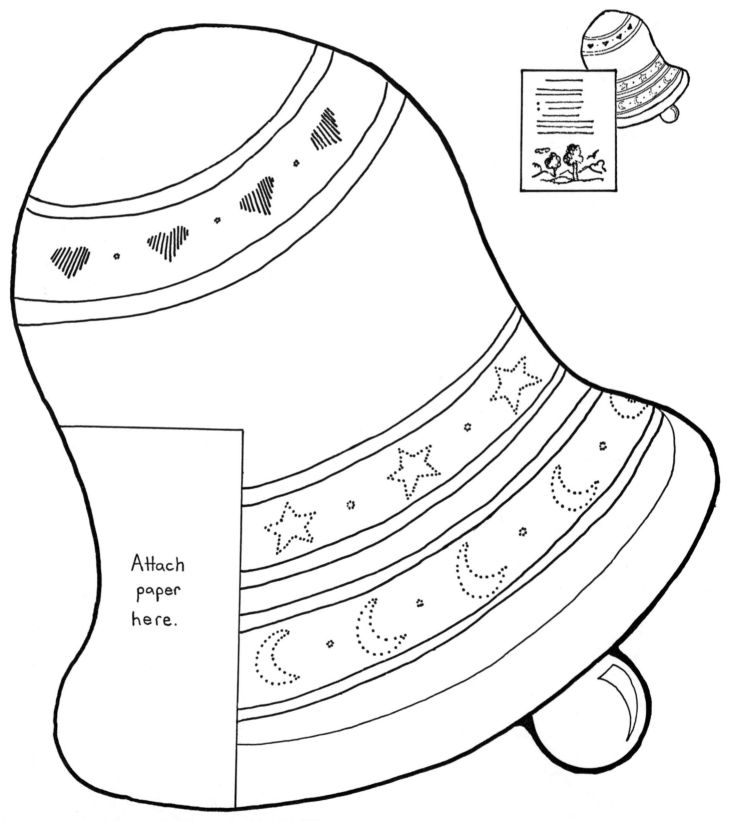

Attach paper here.

RING THE BELL!

Color all of the spaces with words that rhyme with bell.

you

roll

me

sell

fell

ball

yes

tell

well

stop

yell

it

to

bell

girl

Write the rhyming words.

Bell

___ell

___ell

___ell

___ell

___ell

love

the

Recognizing rhyming words
© 1990 by Incentive Publications, Inc., Nashville, TN.

Name _____

COUNT THE BELLS

Cut and paste the number words in the correct boxes.
How many bells are there on this page? _____

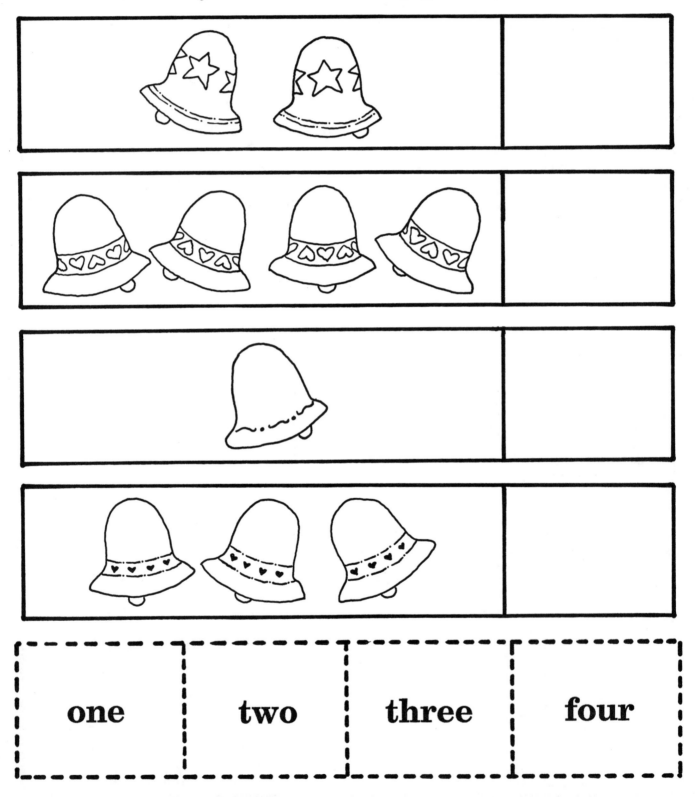

Recognizing number words/counting
© 1990 by Incentive Publications, Inc., Nashville, TN.

POSITIVE COMMUNICATORS

_____ has started off the New Year with a bang!

BANG

_____
signed

_____
date

Fold along the dotted line. Write message inside.

THANK YOU SO MUCH!

TEACHER/PARENT CONFERENCE FORM

Dear _____ ,

    It's conference time again. I am looking forward to the opportunity to talk with you about _____'s progress and ways that we can work together for the good of your child during the rest of the school year.

Please come for a conference on _____ at _____ o'clock.

Sincerely,

_____

- -

Please sign and return.

- -

❑   I can come for a conference on _____ at _____ o'clock.

❑   I cannot come at this time, but I will check with you to set another time.

❑   I especially would like to talk to you about _____

_____

_____

_____
signed

LEARNING TO LISTEN/LISTENING TO LEARN

Major Objective:

Children will develop better listening skills, will come to understand that listening is an important part of the learning process, and will derive pleasure from listening to a variety of sounds.

Things To Do:

- The emphasis on "New Year bells" provides motivation for directing attention to listening. The following activities may be worked in during the month as appropriate to reinforce speaking and listening skills in a natural and meaningful setting.

- Collect different kinds of simple musical instruments (toy drum, violin, recorder, wooden blocks, horn, tambourine, etc.). Arrange the instruments on a table beside a display of animal pictures. (Cut the pictures out of magazines and paste them on construction paper.) Ask the children to experiment with the instruments to see how many different animal sounds they can imitate. (Be sure to properly disinfect the "wind" instruments after each child uses them.) This is a good free time or small group activity.

- Tape various familiar sounds that the children can easily categorize (kitchen sounds, outdoor sounds, playground sounds, etc.). As the children listen to the tape, ask them to identify each sound and tell in what category it belongs.

- Place a different number of beans in each of five small boxes. Ask the children to shake one box at a time and to guess the number of beans in each box by listening to the sound. Open each box and count the beans to check the accuracy of the children's guesses.

- Clap your hands in a pattern (loud, soft, loud, soft, etc.). Then ask the children to repeat the pattern. Increase the length and difficulty of the pattern according to the maturity level of the children.

- Say the following to the children: "I will pronounce four words. Three of the words belong together. One word in the group does not belong. Listen carefully and raise your hand if you can tell which word does not belong in the group." (Examples: salt, pepper, sugar, *spoon*; car, boat, plane, *suitcase*, etc.)

- Read aloud familiar stories, pausing often to ask the children questions. Before beginning to read, ask the children to listen carefully to the story and to be ready to answer your questions. (Example: Read *The Shoemaker And The Elves* , page 75. Ask questions such as these: How many elves made the shoes? Who made clothes for the elves? How many pairs of shoes did the elves make the first night?)

- Tell the children to listen carefully to several phrases and to respond to each by saying *who, what, when* or *where*. (Examples: at ten o'clock (when); in the meadow (where); the big red book (what); Sally's father (who); etc.)

- At the beginning of the day, involve the children in the selection of a "word of the day." Talk about the word and write it on the chalkboard. Whenever someone hears the word, he or she is to clap and say, "I heard the word of the day. _____ just said _____ ." Remember to say the word at unexpected times and to encourage the children to do the same. The word also may be heard in stories, records and songs. Good words to choose include *happy, listen, tell, before, time, after, door* and *school*.

Name _____

HEAR HERE!

Color the pictures of things you can hear.

Decision making

STRIKE UP THE RHYTHM

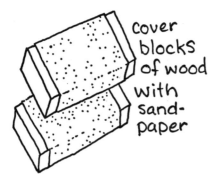 cover
blocks
of wood
with
sand-
paper

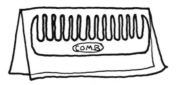 wax paper
wrapped over a comb
makes a good humming
instrument

make cymbals
out of
pan lids

Children will enjoy making and using these simple rhythm band instruments!

Shaker

staple 2 paper plates together & fill with dried beans

Drum

punch holes in an empty oatmeal container

tie string through holes

cover container with inner tube, or balloon rubber & secure with string or strong rubber band

Kazoo

paper towel roll

wax paper

punch a hole with a pencil

Cover end of roll with wax paper secured with a rubber band

THINGS TO LISTEN TO

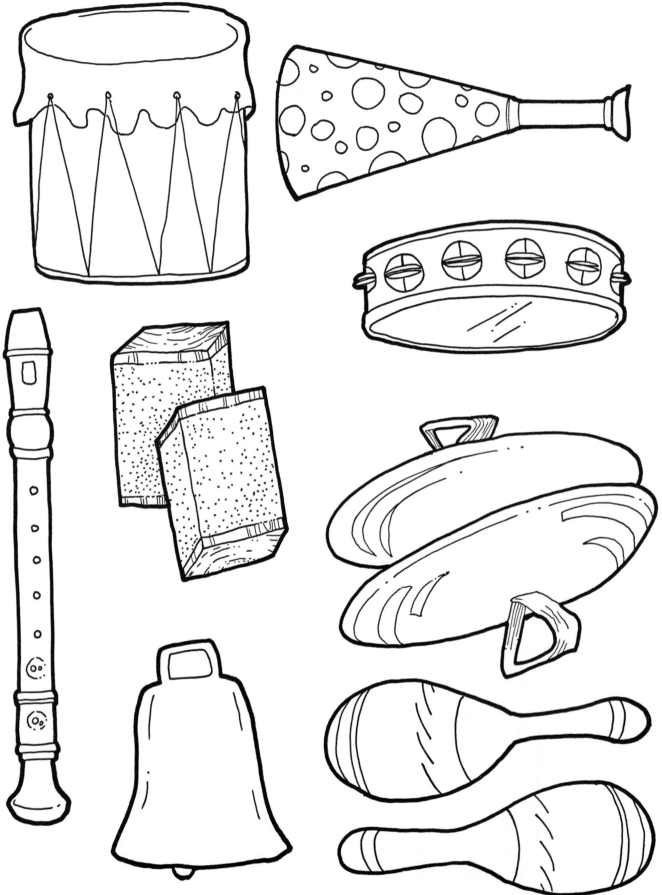

BIRTHDAYS ARE SPECIAL DAYS

Major Objective:

Children will learn the names of the twelve months of the year, will come to understand that the date of birth determines one's age, and will gain reinforcement of their own birth dates and self-concepts.

Things To Do:

- Let the children help plan a birthday party for the entire class! Be sure that the children are assigned individual and group responsibilities as part of the planning (making party favors, decorating the room, folding napkins, setting tables, preparing refreshments, etc.).

Cover two small cardboard boxes with white tissue paper and cut an opening (large enough for an 8 1/2" x 11" piece of paper) in each box. Help the children cut out and color party foods (patterns on page 35) and party favors (patterns on page 36) to paste on the boxes.

Give the children two sheets of construction paper each and provide them with old catalogs and magazines. Ask each child to cut out a picture of a gift he or she would like to receive and a picture of his or her favorite party food. Then direct each child to paste each picture on a sheet of construction paper on which his or her name has been written. Instruct the children to insert their pictures in the appropriate boxes. Open one box at a time and ask each child to come forward, to show his or her chosen gift or food, and to give reasons for the choice.

Play party games and enjoy party refreshments!

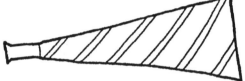

- Read *A Birthday For Frances* (see page 77) to the class. Let the children react to the story as you read. Then, ask the children to express their feelings about Frances' attitude toward the birthday.

- Reproduce the birthday crown on page 37 for each child. Help the children follow the directions to make tissue paper crowns to wear at a class birthday party or during a birthday parade throughout the school.

- To help the children become familiar with the names of the months and days on which their birthdays fall (or are celebrated), conduct the class birthday calendar activity on page 38. Encourage each child to mark the birthdays of family members and friends in this manner at home!

- To enhance self-concept and "the uniqueness of self," reproduce the "I Am Me" banner (page 47) in quantities sufficient to meet the needs of the class. Help the children complete the banners to take home.

- Bake "paintbrush cookies" and make "easy party punch" (see page 48). Or, reproduce the recipe page and send it home with each child as "happy homework" and/or give a copy to each parent at a parent conference. Discuss the meanings of the words *ingredients* and *dissolve* with the children.

- Read *Mr. Rabbit And The Lovely Present* (page 78). After discussion, ask each child to name something that his or her mother would like to receive as a birthday present. Then have the children draw pictures of the gifts and take the pictures home to their mothers!

PARTY FOODS

PARTY FAVORS

My Birthday is _____

I will be _____ years old!

BIRTHDAY CROWN

1. Place the pattern on a piece of construction paper (with the base of the crown touching one edge of the paper).
2. Fold in half.
3. Cut along the top ridges of the crown.
4. Unfold. Fill in the information and decorate the patterns with crayons or markers.
5. Paste or tape the sides of the two patterns together to form a crown.

CLASS BIRTHDAY CALENDAR

What To Use:
large 12-month calendar
birthday tags (page 39)
list of the children's birthdays
tape
scissors

What To Do:
1. Cut the calendar apart and hang the twelve months in sequence at the children's eye level.
2. Reproduce the birthday tags on page 39 in quantities to meet the needs of the class. Let each child select a tag and write his or her name on the tag.
3. Talk about the calendar. Name the months and let the children repeat the names.
4. Ask if anyone can identify his or her birthday. (Check the children's responses with the dates you have written on your birthday chart, see page 40.) If a child's response is correct, let the child attach his or her birthday tag to the calendar on the correct date (removable tape works well).
5. Continue this process until all of the children have identified their birth dates.
6. Then, call the roll and ask each child to say his or her birth date and point to it on the calendar.
7. Conclude the activity by giving each child a birthday bookmark to complete (page 39).

BIRTHDAY TAGS

Bookmark

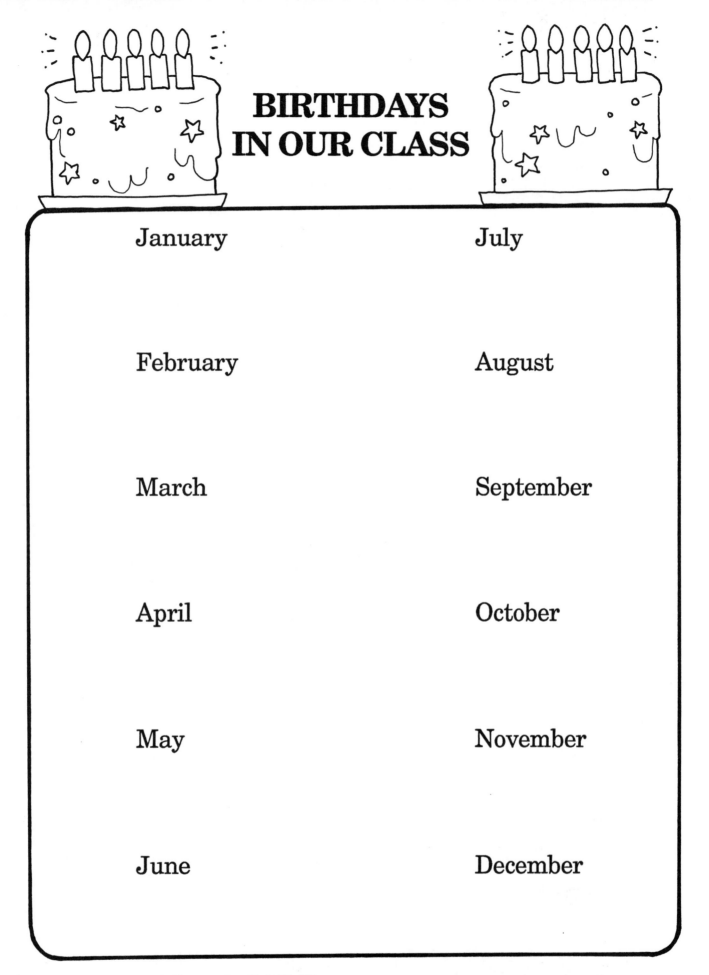

BIRTHDAYS IN OUR CLASS

January	July
February	August
March	September
April	October
May	November
June	December

January Birthdays

MONTHLY HEADINGS

Cut and paste the monthly headings on the birthday banner (page 41) and reproduce the banner for each month of the year. Help the children write their names and birthdays on the appropriate birthday banners. Display the birthday banner each month. Don't forget to hang the summer birthday banners during the last month of school!

February Birthdays

March Birthdays

April Birthdays

May Birthdays

June Birthdays

July Birthdays

August Birthdays

September Birthdays

October Birthdays

November Birthdays

December Birthdays

Name _____

A SILLY PARTY

Circle 6 mistakes.
Color everything but the mistakes.

Visual discrimination/decision making
© 1990 by INCENTIVE PUBLICATIONS, Inc., Nashville, TN.

Name _____

BEST FITS

Circle the gift in each row that best fits in the box.

Visual discrimination
© 1990 by Incentive Publications, Inc., Nashville, TN.

Name _____

COUNT THE CANDLES

Jill is four (4).
Jack is five (5).
Jenny is six (6).
Jimmy is the oldest.
Draw lines to match the children and the birthday cakes.

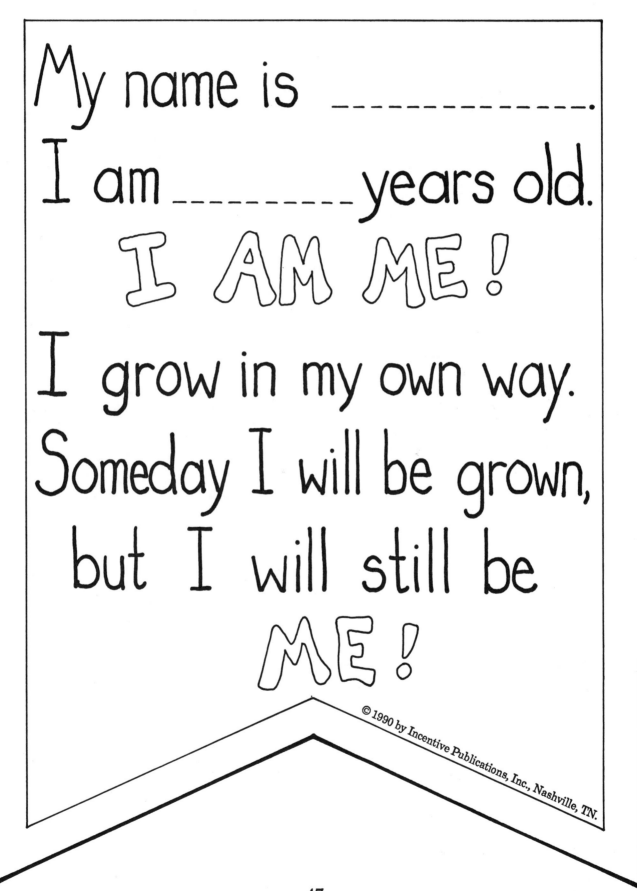

My name is _____.
I am _____ years old.
I AM ME!
I grow in my own way.
Someday I will be grown,
but I will still be
ME!

BIRTHDAY PARTY RECIPES

Paintbrush Cookies

Mix thoroughly in bowl:
1/3 cup sugar
1/3 cup soft shortening
2/3 cup honey
1 egg
1 teaspoon vanilla

Stir together in another bowl:
2 3/4 cups flour
1 teaspoon soda
1 teaspoon salt

1. Mix dry ingredients into shortening mixture. Chill 1 hour.
2. Heat oven to 375º. Lightly grease baking sheet.
3. Divide chilled dough into 3 portions. (Put 2 portions in refrigerator until ready to use.)
4. On lightly floured board, roll dough to 1/4 inch thickness. Cut into different shapes. Place on prepared baking sheet.
5. With small paintbrushes, paint designs on cookies with egg yolk paint (divide mixture of 1 egg yolk and 1/4 teaspoon water among small cups — add food coloring to each cup.)
6. Bake 8 to 10 minutes. Let cookies cool about 2 minutes on baking sheet. Then cool on wire rack.

Makes 5 dozen.

Easy Party Punch

1 cup water
1 qt. orange juice
3 fresh lemons

1/2 cup sugar
1 qt. cranberry juice
1 qt. pineapple juice

1. Mix sugar, water and juice of 3 lemons until sugar dissolves.
2. Add orange, cranberry and pineapple juice. Stir well.

Makes about 24 servings.

SNOW AND ICE AND FREEZING COLD

Major Objective:
Children will develop appreciation for the differences between cold and warm climates and will learn about cold weather and the appropriate dress for cold and wintry conditions.

Things To Do:

- Even children who live in warm climates will enjoy learning about snow and ice and freezing cold. Thinking about cold weather and the need for warm clothing provides readiness for the study of clothing (pages 63 - 76). Many of the activities in these two units may be combined or used interchangeably.

- Let the children make torn-paper winter pictures. Provide dark blue construction paper, white tissue paper and paste. Instruct the children to tear the paper into pieces of different shapes and sizes and to arrange the pieces on dark blue backgrounds to form snowy day scenes. Discuss things they can add to their scenes such as snowmen, igloos, snowflakes, icicles, snow-laden trees, etc. Remember, no scissors allowed!

- Read and enjoy the pictures in *The Snowy Day* by Ezra Jack Keats (see page 78).

- Discuss colds and sore throats and their causes and treatments. Inform the children of the need to cover their mouths when they cough and to wash their hands often with soap and water to prevent the transmission of germs. Remind the children that they should stay home when they are sick. As a follow-up, discuss the reasons why warm, water-proof clothing should be worn in snowy weather. Emphasize the need to wear boots, hats, mufflers and gloves or mittens.

Use activities from the "Learning About Clothing" unit (pages 63 - 76) for reinforcement. Provide large sheets of paper and crayons for the children to use to draw cold weather outfits.

49

Construction:
1. Label one half of the board "Hot Climates" and the other half "Cold Climates."
2. Provide the children with old magazines and calendar pictures. Ask the children to cut out pictures of people in hot and cold climates. Discuss the meaning of the word *climate*. Then help the children decide on which side of the board their pictures belong.
3. Reproduce the cold and hot climate borders (pages 51 and 52) in quantities to meet the needs of the class. Have the children color the borders and attach them to their pictures. Display the pictures on the board.

Use:
Use the board as a springboard for discussion of...
- how climate affects plants and animals
- how and why people who live in hot climates have different homes, hobbies and clothing than people who live in cold climates
- where some of the hottest and coldest places in the world are located
- what kind of climate your community is located in

After several days of discussion and related activities, have the children draw pictures of themselves in the kinds of climates in which they would like to live. Add the drawings to the board.

Note: Pages 51 and 52 also may be used to frame the children's drawings, to "show off" other activity sheets, to decorate desks and to recognize accomplishments!

COLD CLIMATE BORDER

Attach paper here.

1. Reproduce the border pattern on heavy white paper.
2. Color and cut out the border.
3. Attach a special paper or project to the border.

HOT CLIMATE BORDER

Attach paper here.

1. Reproduce the border pattern on heavy white paper.
2. Color and cut out the border.
3. Attach a special paper or project to the border.

Name _____

HOT OR COLD

Write the temperature that each thermometer shows.

Draw a picture beside each thermometer
to "match" the temperature.

20°F

100 °F

Reading thermometers/making associations
© 1990 by Incentive Publications, Inc., Nashville, TN.

Name _____

I LOVE A SNOWY DAY

Use blue, green, brown and white crayons to color this snowy day picture.

Draw yourself and a friend doing something you would like to do on a snowy day.

Relating to weather conditions
© 1990 by Incentive Publications, Inc., Nashville, TN.

Name _____

A SNOWY DAY

Color the pictures and tell the story.

Name _____

SNOWMAN SHAPES

Cut and paste the numerals in the correct boxes.

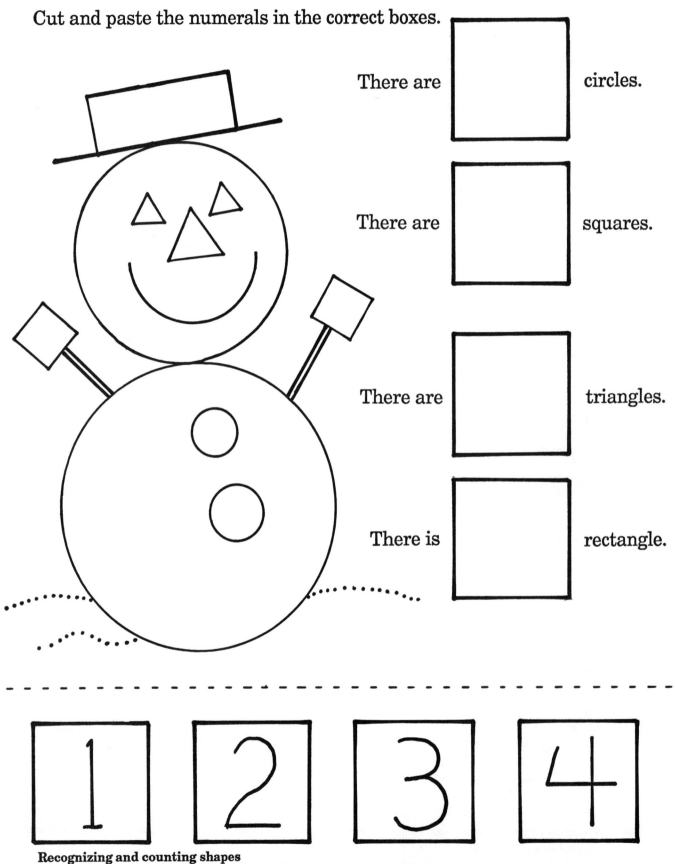

There are ☐ circles.

There are ☐ squares.

There are ☐ triangles.

There is ☐ rectangle.

1   2   3   4

Recognizing and counting shapes
© 1990 by Incentive Publications, Inc., Nashville, TN.

SNOW PUZZLERS

1. Reproduce the puzzles below in quantities to meet the needs of the class.
2. Cut the puzzles apart and put a set of puzzles in an envelope for each child.
3. Have the children match each picture with the correct word.

Note: The snow puzzles also can be used as an independent free-time or take-home activity.

POSITIVE BEHAVIOR AWARDS

Dear _____ ,

You made your teacher proud
today because _____

_____

_____ .

_____
signed

_____
date

GOOD WORKER AWARD

To: _____

For: _____

_____
signed

_____
date

DON'T FORGET THE BIRDS

Help the children make these easy bird feeders. Hang the feeders outside a classroom window and watch for the birds!

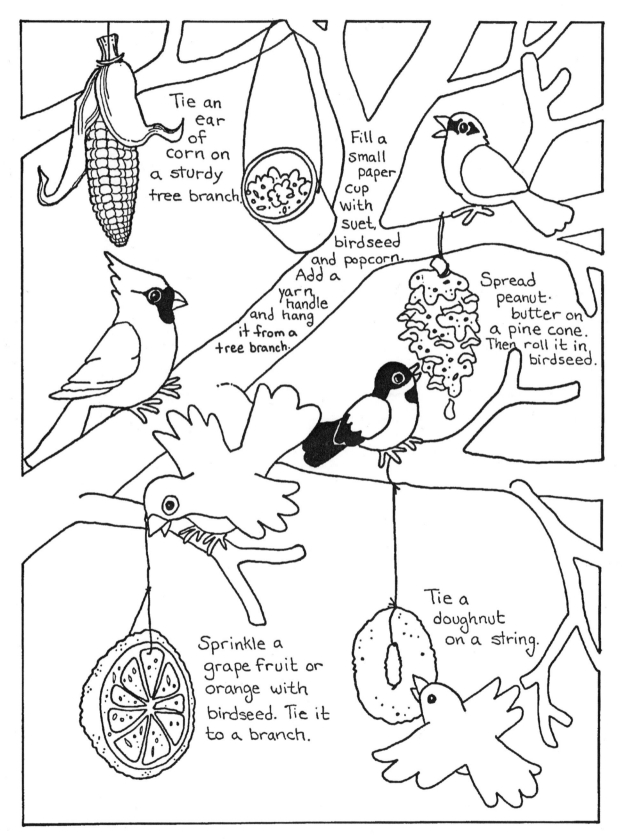

Tie an ear of corn on a sturdy tree branch.

Fill a small paper cup with suet, birdseed and popcorn. Add a yarn handle and hang it from a tree branch.

Spread peanut butter on a pine cone. Then roll it in birdseed.

Sprinkle a grape fruit or orange with birdseed. Tie it to a branch.

Tie a doughnut on a string.

SCIENCE EXPERIMENTS WITH ICE

Find Out:
Does ice melt more quickly in
the sunlight than it does in the shade?
If so, why?

What To Use:
2 sheet of dark construction paper
2 trays or cookie sheets
6 ice cubes
(You will need a sunny window and a
shaded area.)

What To Do:
1. Place three ice cubes on each sheet of paper and place each paper on a tray or
   cookie sheet.
2. Place one tray in a sunny window and the other tray in a shaded area.
3. Check the trays periodically to see which ice cubes melt more quickly.

Findings:
Ice melts more quickly in the sunlight than it does in the shade because the sun
gives off heat.

Find Out:
Do ice cubes float in water?

What To Use:
1 glass
2 ice cubes
water

What To Do:
1. Place two ice cubes in a glass.
2. Pour water into the glass to cover the ice
   cubes.
3. Observe that the ice cubes float to the top of
   the water.

Findings:
Ice cubes float in water because they are lighter
than water. Icicles are lighter than rain or snow.

WINTER PATTERNS

SNOWY DAY PATTERNS

LEARNING ABOUT CLOTHING

Major Objective:
Children will become familiar with various kinds of materials used to make clothing, will learn to identify the origin of materials (plant, animal, man-made), and will learn to choose clothing appropriate for various climates and occasions.

Things To Do:

- Reproduce the puppet and clothing patterns on pages 67 - 70 in quantities to meet the needs of the class. Instruct the children to color the patterns and to paste the clothes on the puppets. Help the children paste or staple their puppets on popsicle sticks. Then, seat the children in a circle. Ask them to hold their puppets until they are called. Instruct each child to pretend that his or her voice is the voice of the puppet. Call upon one child at a time and ask the child to stand, to show his or her puppet and to tell at least two things about the clothing the puppet is wearing. Prompt the children if necessary.

- Mount pictures of many kinds of clothing on index cards. Cut pictures representing the four seasons out of magazines and paste these on cardboard. Tape the season cards to the board. Show the children one clothing card at a time and ask them to tell during which season that piece of clothing would be worn. Tape the clothing pictures below the appropriate season pictures.

- Collect as many different kinds of hats as you can and place them in a large box. Let the children take turns closing their eyes, reaching into the box and picking a hat. Ask each child to place the hat on his or her head and to "act out" the character who might wear the hat.

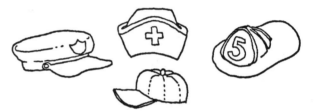

- Reinforce clothing identification, increase color awareness, develop attention spans and provide personal recognition by having the children "line up" for activities or events as you call for...
    all those wearing green socks
    all those wearing red shirts
    etc.
Continue in this manner until all of the children have been called.

- Ask someone who sews to present a demonstration of how a simple article of clothing is made. Ask several volunteers to help the children make a simple dress, shirt or pants for a doll, stuffed animal, or paper doll (see pages 67-69).

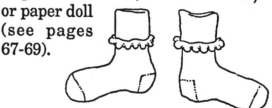

- Invite the owner of a local children's clothing store to visit the class. Ask the guest to discuss how they decide what to buy for the store, where and when they go to market, how they draw customers into the store, and what happens to the clothing that does not sell. This may sound a bit overwhelming, but if the guest is advised of the children's level of understanding, this can be a meaningful lesson in consumer education.

- Assemble a collection of mail order catalogs containing children's clothes. Encourage the children to browse through the catalogs during their free time. At an appointed time, discuss styles, prices, colors, fabrics and the suitability of various clothes for different climates and lifestyles.

- Ask the children to name ways that clothing may be fastened (buckles, zippers, shoelaces, buttons, snaps, hooks and eyes, Velcro, etc.). Then say, "Everyone who is wearing buttons please stand up." Continue in this manner, substituting different fasteners each time. Examine the various fasteners on the children's clothing and discuss the importance of being able to fasten your own clothing without help.

- Make a "feeling box" to help the children learn to identify and describe a variety of fabrics from which clothing is made. Cut a hole in one end of a shoe box (large enough for a child's hand) and place swatches of fabric inside the box. Have one child at a time reach inside the box, feel a swatch of fabric and identify the fabric (without looking at it!).

- Reproduce the clothing pairs on page 71. Cut the pairs apart and paste each picture on a 5" x 7" index card. Use the cards to play a matching game (follow the rules of the card game "Old Maid"). In order to have an "odd" card for the last player to be "out," delete one card. Use the cards for other matching games. Have the children draw one card each. The children having matching pairs may be partners for a specific play time or work activity. Or, have the children draw cards and describe a person who might wear the article of clothing pictured on each card.

- Provide all shapes and sizes of fabric scraps. Have the children paste the scraps on sheets of construction paper to make collages.

- Fill a clothes basket with clothes of two sizes — too big and too small. Have a modeling session during which each child tries on an item of clothing and identifies it as "too big" or "too small."

Construction:

1. Cut out pictures of plants and animals from which we get raw materials for clothing and a picture of a group of people. Mount the pictures on cardboard.

2. Cut the caption "Where Do Clothes Come From?" out of construction paper and attach it to the board.

3. Divide the board into two sides. Cut the headings "Plants & Animals" and "Made By Man" out of construction paper and attach them to the board as shown.

4. Display the mounted pictures on the appropriate sides of the board.

5. Pin an envelope containing swatches of various clothing materials to the board.

6. Discuss with the children the possible origin of each kind of material. Be sure to relate the discussion to clothes that the children are wearing.

7. As a group, identify the side of the board on which each swatch belongs. Ask a child to tack the swatches to the board.

8. Leave the swatches in place to be manipulated by the children. Review and replace the swatches with the total group periodically until the children can easily identify the materials and classify them correctly.

PAPER DOLL RELAY

What To Use:
flannel board
felt numbers 1 - 10
two paper dolls (boy & girl, 3 feet each)
several items of clothing for each doll

What To Do:
1. Cut two large paper dolls (a boy and girl) out of poster board, cardboard or other sturdy paper. (Hint: Trace around a child to make the paper dolls!)
2. Place the two dolls at the front of the room.
3. Divide the children into two teams. Assign one doll to each team.
4. Tell the children that they are going to have a relay contest to see which team can dress its doll first.
5. Place a series of sequential numbers (2, 3, 4, etc.) on a flannel board. Then call on a member of team 1 to add the next number in the sequence. If the child can do this correctly, he or she may put one article of clothing on the team's doll. If not, a member of team 2 can try to complete the number sequence.
6 Continue in this manner, alternating teams, until one doll is completely dressed. The team who dresses its doll first is the winner!

66

BOY PAPER DOLL

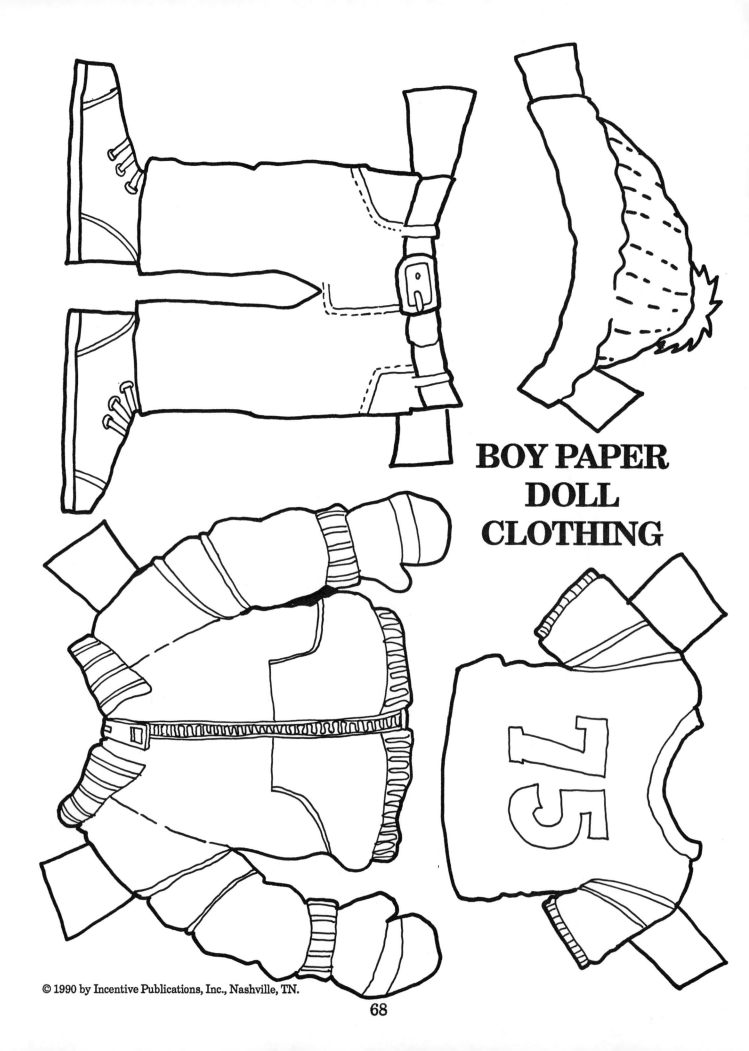

BOY PAPER DOLL CLOTHING

**GIRL
PAPER
DOLL**

GIRL PAPER DOLL CLOTHING

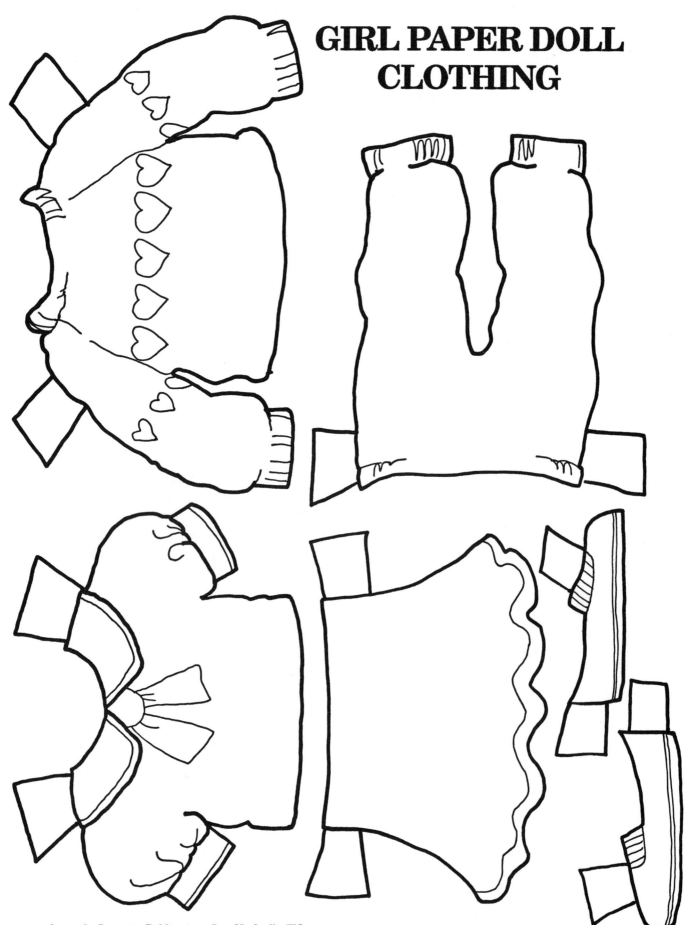

CLOTHING PAIRS

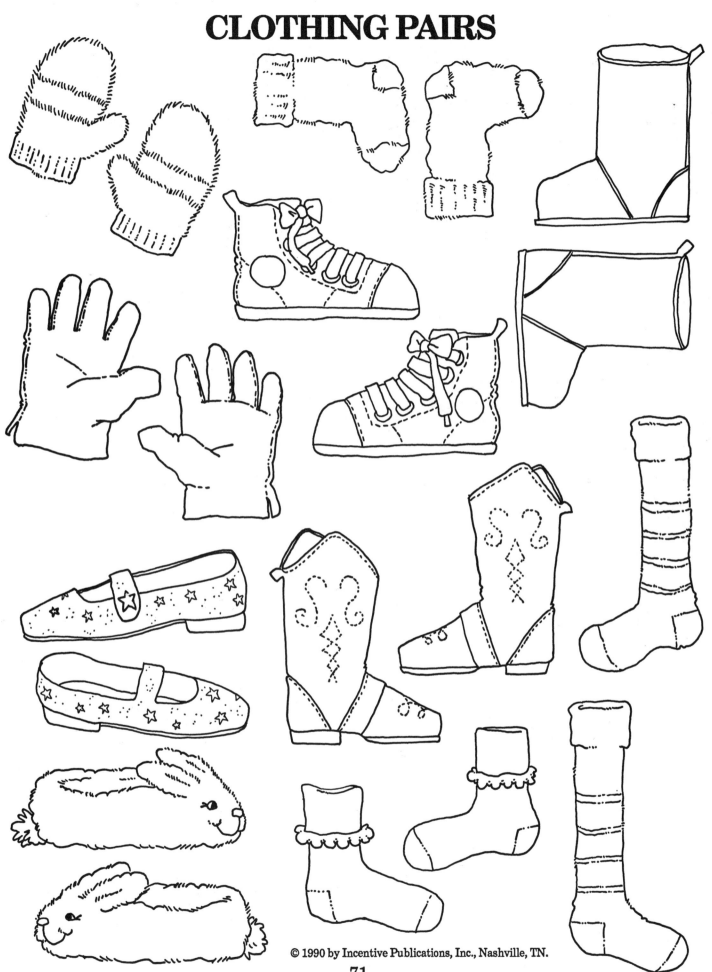

Name _____

TELL TALE CLOTHES

Some people wear hats and uniforms that help us know what kind
of work they do.
Cut and paste the hats in the correct boxes.

Picture/idea association
© 1990 by Incentive Publications, Inc., Nashville, TN.

HATS TO DRAW

Draw a hat for each person.

Susan is five years old.
She lives in a cold climate.
She needs a hat to keep her ears
    warm.

Mrs. Brown is Susan's grandmother.
She wears pretty clothes.
She would like a fancy hat
    for tea parties.

Ms. Jones is Susan's teacher.
She has always wanted a straw
    hat.

Sammie is Susan's brother.
He is older than Susan.
He wants a cowboy hat.

Mental imagery
© 1990 by Incentive Publications, Inc., Nashville, TN.

READ AND DO

Draw boots on the cowboy.
Color the tallest boy's shirt red.
Color the flower on the smallest girl's hat yellow.
Color the baby's shirt blue.

Following directions
© 1990 by Incentive Publications, Inc., Nashville, TN.

THE SHOEMAKER AND THE ELVES

Once upon a time there lived an honest shoemaker and his kind wife. The shoemaker worked very hard, but he never could make enough shoes to buy anything but the poorest food and clothing.

One night the shoemaker cut his last pair of shoes from the only piece of leather he owned. The next morning he couldn't believe his eyes when he saw two beautiful shoes on his workbench. It wasn't long before a traveler came along and bought the shoes.

With great joy the shoemaker rushed out to buy leather to make two pairs of shoes, a chicken to make stew and flour to make bread. As he cut out the shoes, his wife prepared stew and bread to leave on the workbench beside the shoes. When they awoke the next morning, they danced for joy to find two pairs of shiny new shoes on the workbench.

The same thing happened for several nights. One night they decided to hide and watch to see who was making the shoes. They fell asleep and were awakened by the tapping of two tiny hammers. Two elves were working away and, in no time, had made eight pairs of shoes!

After the elves left, the wife went to her trunk and pulled out a piece of velvet she had been saving. She sewed until morning. Then she placed two fine little suits and matching hats on the workbench.

The next night she and her husband hid again. They could hardly keep quiet as they watched the elves put on their new clothes and dance out the door.

The shoemaker and his wife watched for many nights, but the elves never came again. Even so, the people in the village were amazed by the good fortune that had come to the shoemaker and his wife. The couple never had to go to bed hungry again.

THIS IS THE WAY WE WASH OUR CLOTHES

Lead the children in singing *This Is The Way We Wash Our Clothes* (sung to the tune of *Here We Go 'Round The Mulberry Bush*). Have the children make the appropriate motions as they sing each verse. Then let the children add their own verses and motions.

This is the way we wash our clothes

wash our clothes wash our clothes.

This is the way we wash our clothes so

ear – ly in the morn – ing.

This is the way we...

... iron our clothes

... hang our clothes

... tie our shoes

... button our shirts

... zip our boots

... model our clothes

BIBLIOGRAPHY

Beginning To Learn About Winter. Richard L. Allington. Raintree Children's Books.
A pictorial portrayal of the marvels of the coldest season goes well beyond snow and slush.

A Birthday For Frances. Russell Hoban. Harper & Row.
Frances' jealousy causes her to sing "Happy Birthday" to an imaginary Alice on her little sister Gloria's birthday.

Happy New Year 'Round The World. Lois S. Johnson. Rand McNally & Co.
A good teacher's reference for the traditions, customs and history of new year celebrations around the world.

How To Keep Warm In Winter. David Ross. Thomas Y. Crowell.
A collection of fun approaches to warm-ups, cool maneuvers, energy conservation, winter fashion hints, cold weather inventions and more!

If There Were Dreams To Sell. Compiled by Barbara Lalicki. Lothrop, Lee & Shepard.
A most unusual collection of verses from Mother Goose, Dickinson, Keats and others. All are beautifully presented to magically capture seasonal scenes just as they are about to spring into life.

Let's Discover Winter Woods. Ada and Frank Graham, Jr. Golden Press.
This Audubon Primer series book is designed to focus on one particular aspect of the natural world. Vivid full-color photographs present the adventures of real children and the discoveries they make in winter woods.

Let's Find Out About New Year's Day. Martha and Charles Shapp. Franklin Watts.
A lively account of New Year's Day celebrations as observed by different people at different times, in different ways and in different languages.

A Letter To Amy. Ezra Jack Keats. Harper & Row.
This is the story of the progression of a birthday party invitation written for a friend.

The Snowy Day. Ezra Jack Keats. Viking Press.
An all-time favorite picture book shows how one little boy finds many creative ways to entertain himself on a snowy day.

Stopping By Woods On A Snowy Evening. Robert Frost. Holt, Rinehart & Winston, Inc.
Susan Jeffers' beautiful illustrations portray a wonderful snowy day experience that will delight children.

The Story Of Our Calendar. Ruth Brindze. The Vanguard Press, Inc.
This is a good teacher resource for information related to the development and significance of the calendar in world history.

A Time To Keep. Tasha Tudor. Rand McNally & Co.
A grandmother's accounting of year-round holiday celebrations from days gone by is accompanied by captivating illustrations with an old fashioned flavor.

A Walk In The Snow. Phyllis S. Busch. J.B. Lippincott.
Black and white photographic illustrations highlight the many wonders of a snowy day. This is a good reference book for the reading table during a winter weather study.

What Will You Do Here All Winter? Charles Martin. Green Willow Press.
The captivating story of all kinds of things a family can do on an island during long winter days.

Why Won't Winter Go. Lisa McLaughlin. Lothrop, Lee & Shepard.
Andy is bored with winter until his sister Meg shows him that snowy days can be fun. This easy-to-read picture book will brighten a cold, cold day.

Winter Book. Harriett Webster. Charles Scribner's Sons.
Chapters 1 - 4 contain a wealth of fun activities to enrich and strengthen winter day programs. (A good teacher resource.)

A Year Of Beasts. Ashley Wolff. E.P. Dutton, Inc.
A brother and sister observe many different field and forest animals around their country home through the year.

INDEX